36 Laws of Powder

Book written by Leroy A Gordon 2/26/14

36 Laws of Powder is a book of knowledge that I had collected over the years from myself and other hustlers that I've dealt with in the past. I decided to put together a book of rules and regulations that, me and a few of my hustling friends once lived by, while dealing powder cocaine. The book is filled with information on how we managed to maintain a drug dealing life style, while keeping a low-key profile as tax paying citizens at the same time.

Every hustler has their own set of rules that they live by, but unfortunately some of those hustlers ended up behind bars with long lengthy prison sentences, with nothing to show from their days of hustling. The drug game isn't about how much money you got, it's about how long you last. Some last a few years, some last a few months, and some last a few days.

36 laws of powder guided me as a hustler, into the right direction to where I could quit the game and become a tax paying citizens. A lot of big corporations were built on drug funds and

they were very successful. They were successful because they set laws and regulations for themselves as well, by keeping a low-key profile and knowing when to stop.

A lot of critics would say that this book is teaching criminals how to break the law, or that I'm glorifying selling drugs. I'm just giving them the blue print on how some of us were able to get out of the game successfully, and how we became legitimate tax paying citizens as businessmen.

Just like the bible, it has a lot of bad thinks inside of it, but it was written for you to learn from others mistakes by taking the good from it. Not that I'm comparing the bible to my book, but to us it as an example that all good books has a little bad mixed in with the good. I'm now a man of GOD and this is my way of getting the hustlers attention, to get them onto the right path and into the Kingdom of the Lord.

My Introduction

As a teenager I learned a lot about the drug game growing up in the projects. I remember being poor and living in a single parent house hold with my two sisters, and there wasn't a father around to look up to that could teach me what's right from wrong. A new pair of shoes when I was coming up as a kid was a privilege, and wearing designer clothes was a dream. I can recall having two pair of pants to my name, and having to rotate them throughout the week, for the entire school year. The fact that I had to wear the same two pair of jeans the entire school year, was my reason for dropping out of school.

As a kid living in the projects sitting on my front porch looking for a way out, I had no doctors and lawyers to look up to. I had no idea that I could become something positive, because all I saw was drug dealers who were living the American dream. Once I learned how to hustle, my life changed and so did my life style. I went from not having anything to having everything I wanted, and it became an addiction.

My love for wealth drove me to wanting to sell more drugs, because selling drugs was the only way to be successful in my neighborhood. We all wanted to live that American dream, but none of us had an out plan. A lot of the hustlers from my neighborhood ending up selling drugs until they were dead or in jail, and none of them owned anything.

We threw our money away like it was the morning trash, because we had little respect for it because it was so easy to get. I can recall one of my best friends having so much money, that he would bring out a zip lock bag filled with five dollar bills. He would make sure every bill was gone by the time he went in for the night, because that was his way of getting rid of the small bills. He had so much money that he would spend five dollar bills for about two years straight, and he told me if he made it to the hundred dollar bills he was going broke. After being around him for a 2 year period, I never saw him with a ten dollar bill, that's how long his money was.

We thought it was best to spend, than to save and invest, because we were too afraid that the police would lock us up if we invested money into a business. Our minds was dumb founded about how to invest out money without running our selves hot, but what we didn't realize was, we were already running our selves hot by buying all the flashy cars and jewelry.

A lot of the hustlers today don't have morals and respect for others. They like to talk down on those that are less fortune and degrade women by pouring champagne on them in strip clubs, as they shower them with singles. Hustling use to be about getting you and your family out of a bad situation, and putting them into a better situation. Now it's all about them, and treating a woman they just met, better than they treat their own mothers, who gave them life.

Hustlers now days think it's all about whom got more than the other, instead of helping the community grow as one. I know I just hit a nerve with that one, because I know some of you are probable thinking "how can anyone help the community by selling drugs". Just like people give back to the community that owners a liquor store, a gun store, a drug store, a bar-b-q pit, legal weed shops and stores that sells cigarettes and sugar to the people, which most of those businesses kills more people than cocaine does.

The only difference between cocaine and other businesses is, the government considers cocaine as being legal. Sugar is more of an addiction than cocaine, and it is the number one cause of obesity and diabetes. I never been addicted to cocaine, but I'm addicted to sugar. I can't go a day without eating sugar, and its making my chances of dying sooner before my time high.

The little girl scouts outside the grocery stores are like crack dealers, I can't walk pass them without buying two to three boxes of girls scout cookies. Cocaine was once an ingredient used by a soda company, until they realized it was causing people to be addicted to it. The same thing with sugar, but they haven't banned it yet. From a (CNN) report -- Sugar-sweetened beverages are linked to more than 180,000 obesity-related deaths worldwide each year, according to new research presented this week at an American Heart Association conference. "This means about one in every 100 deaths from obesity-related diseases is caused by drinking sugary beverages," says study author Gitanjali Singh, a postdoctoral research fellow at the Harvard School of Public Health. Among the world's 35 largest countries, Mexico had the highest death rates from sugary drinks, and Bangladesh had the lowest, according to the study. The United States ranked third.

I'm not trying to glorify selling cocaine; I'm just making a point. I just know that people are going to deal it no matter what, because there's always going to be a big demand for it. I'm just giving those who do sell it a proper way to do it, and turn it into something positive.

Cocaine has been around for a long time and it's not going anywhere, because it's a strong addiction like sugar. Some people can't leave without it, and it helps them deal with certain problems and situations in their life. So if they're going to sell it regardless because of the high demands, I feel like as an ex-drug dealer, I could help them set an end point and become a successful businessman. Instead of selling drugs for ever until they're serving a life sentence or dead.

A lot of American businesses were built on blood money; some were built on slavery, murder, robbery, distortion, sex, racism, and drugs. So don't act as if I doing something wrong, when I could just sit back and do nothing, and they're still going to sell it. Even God's solders in the bible did dirty for a good cause.

If the government made cocaine legal today, this topic wouldn't be discussed. So what we are saying is, as long as a bunch of old guys on Capitol Hill say it's not right, it's not right. But once they say it is, it is. And we all know that their yes, is only a yes if it benefits them.

What If the government passed a bill that made sugar illegal tomorrow, would I be wrong for speaking on the behalf of sugar companies? Farmers would lose money and a lot of people would lose jobs, which would cause a big impact on our economy. People would stand up and fight for sugar companies to save jobs, even though it's a product that's killing a lot of people.

I'm not saying that selling cocaine is right, and that it should be legal. I think it's wrong, but I know there are people in poverty neighborhoods like the one I grew up in, are going to sell it no matter what. I was once them, and I know how hard it is to not sell it when the opportunity is in your face 24/7.

I just want to give them an out game and make a negative situation into a positive situation, because some wrongs can be made right.

Law 1- Create aliases

Revelation (20:15) if anyone's name was not found written in the book of life, he was thrown into the lake of fire. The main reason why I created several aliases for myself is, because I didn't want my government name connected to anything I was doing illegal. The drug game is a business that will carry your name as far as your drugs reaches, because drug dealers have a thing for telling other dealers who they cop their drugs from.

Having a well-known name in the drug game is bad business, and it could hurt you in the long run. The better your product is, the bigger your name gets. First your name will start ringing throughout the neighborhood, then the city and then all over the state. Once your name makes it outside of your state and into other states, your name is now in a league of its own. That's when then federal agents will start collaborating with other agents in different states to build a case against you. That's one of the reasons why I made sure ever state I was connected to, knew me by a different alias.

People would be discussing me like I was four different people, because they had no idea that all four of those names was me. I remember a situation where the feds was asking someone about P-Gates and Pistol, not knowing they were the same person. Informants had all four of my aliases circulating throughout the system as different individuals. My drug connect knew me as one thing, my middle man knew me as another, and I never used the same name with females. They all knew me by different names, because that would cut out a lot of name dropping amongst a group of people, which could lead to indictment charges. The authorities would ask drug dealers for information on other drug dealers, whenever they had busted them.

The information would be part of a plea deal to lower their drug charges. If the agents gets a name that matched the names that were given to them by other drug dealers, they could start building a case on that name. But if each dealer is throwing out different names, it's hard for the agents to figure out who's who. Every drug package has a name attached to it, just like the product you see in your local grocery stores. Drug addicts like to associate their drugs with its dealer, because that's how they determine who has the best product. That dealers name would reach as far as his product goes, which will one day end up in the authorities hands on a silver platter.

So the lesser anyone one knows your true identity, the better off you'll be. Not only is it dangerous for the authorities to know your identity, but the robbers as well. The robbers are just has dangerous as the authorities are, because if your name circulates amongst them it could cause some serious problems. If the robbers get word of your name as having money or drugs, they're coming for it without a doubt. The difference is, the feds will give you a life sentence and the robbers will take your life. So if there's a bunch of aliases floating around town, you're most likely to have people's minds boggled, trying to figure out who's who.

Like for instant, I can recall a story about three robbers plotting on a certain individual, and they had told another well-known robber about the plot. They had no idea that the well-known robber was related to the individual they were plotting on, because they didn't know his other alias. Once the well-known robber figured out the plot was intended for his cousin, things went sour real fast. The well-known robber informed his cousin on the plot, and they both setup a booby trap for the robbers to walk into, which ended very badly for the robbers. What I'm trying to show you, is a prime example of how using several different aliases could work into your favorite, because those guys would've never mentioned the plot to the other robber if they had any idea the individual was his cousin.

Having different aliases can also help you with your women situations as well, because female's likes to throw your name under the bus to the authorities once they find out you're messing with another female. That's why it's best to have more than one alias, so when they do, the authorities want have a clue about who she's talking about. Plus females like to name drop amongst other females also, especially if the person is known for having a lot of money. Law 1 is a very important law to live by when you're doing anything illegal, because putting a name to a face is a big factor for building a major case.

LAW 2- Plan an out game

Since I first got into the drug game, I told myself, I don't plan on selling drugs forever. Most hustlers get into the game for the money, but then it becomes a never ending race to the money. They get greedy for wanting more money, not knowing when enough is enough. (1 John 2:15-17) Do not love the world or the things in the world. If anyone loves the world, the love of the Father is not in him. For all that is in the world—the desires of the flesh and the desires of the eyes and pride in possessions—is not from the Father but is from the world. And the world is passing away along with its desires, but whoever does the will of God abides forever.

First we started off as wanting to make a few dollars just to get by, and then that turns into wanting thousands to buy a new car. After we get a new car, we begin to want a couple more cars, which lead us to wanting to buy a house. Now thousands isn't enough, because our appetites done got bigger, now we need millions to do what we desire. You'll find yourself, spoiling yourself to the point where there's no limit to the amount of money you want. Once you get to that point, you're headed for self-destruction. The grave yard or the prison will be your only destination, because getting out of the game would become impossible.

First reason for not getting out of the game is the money, and the second reason is the responsibility of people that depends on you. You have your connect flooding you with endless amount of drugs, that you feel obligated to sell. You have family and friend that you provide for that depends on you, and then you have customers that you feel obligated to keep supplying, because they depend on you as well.

The feeling of knowing people need you is a gift and a curse, because it's a wonderful feeling to feel needed and it's also a major stress to have everyone depending on you. Having to satisfy others plays a big part to why a lot of dealers can't stop selling drugs. They feel like if they stop their letting a lot of people down, which cause them to continue selling until they are dead or in prison, and the sad part about it is everyone else will enjoy the benefits more than the dealer would.

Selling drugs is stressful and even though you have all the money in the world you will never enjoy it, because you never know when the laws or the robbers will catch up with you. While everybody else is having a ball with the money you put your life on the line to earn, you're the only one that's going to have to face the consequences in the end. That's why it's important to plan you an out game, so that you don't have to sell drugs for the rest of your life. Tell yourself that selling drugs is just a temporary hustle to make seed money for what you really want to do. Selling drugs shouldn't be your life time job; it should be a job to help start you a better life.

When you come in the game, you should look at it as if you were playing a basketball game. You play the game until that clock runs out, because if you don't have a timer, you'll play forever until you fall out. That's why you should set yourself a timer, so that you'll know when to stop before you hurt yourself.

All my friends who are serving life sentences didn't have an out game. A lot of people would ask me why my friend's didn't take all that money they made and start a business, and then get out the game. Those people don't realize that selling drugs was considered as being a business to them. When you're making thousands of dollars a day, what business can they create that will bring in those figures. Any business beside that would seem like a waste of their time, because the numbers wouldn't add up. That's why in Law 4 I explained why starting a small business is very important, because it will play a big part in your out game.

Most dealers spend the rest of their lives in prison saying to them self, I should've done this or I should've done that. That's why it's very important that you quit, because selling drugs isn't something you can do forever. A dealer is lucky to have a 6 month run, because that's the average time period for a drug dealer to last in the game. In the drug game, 6 month will seem like a long time. Only a few will see a year or two, and you should be on your hands and knees thinking GOD if you made it past 3 years, because that's a blessing to survive the game that long without getting busted.

Law 3- consignment

My first kilo of cocaine was on consignment, and I would break it down into ounces. I was serving everything from ounces to grams, because I was all about the profit and not how fast I could move it. My motto was "damn right I'm going to take my time, if I get caught with this brick he wouldn't take my time".

The dude who fronted me my first brick on consignment, use to complain about me taking too long. I wasn't trying to impress him on how quick I could flip the brick of cocaine, because I knew by the time I was finished, I could afford my own kilo of cocaine. So if he decided to cut me off, I was already prepared for it. I was all about stacking, because you never know when that dark cloud will rain on your parade.

It's always best to take the consignment, just in case there's a problem with the product making its way to its destination. That way your own money want be affected by the setback of the product getting confiscated by the authorities. Because your drug supplier has more dope than you can imagine, and they will continue sending dope as long as they have someone that's going to move it.

I never would tie my money up into the product, because you're taking a risk of losing every dollar you earned over the period of hustling. Because if something goes wrong with the shipping you'll lost everything you worked hard for, and you'll never have anything to fall back on. It's all about stacking your profit and spending less you can, because you're setting yourself up for the out game.

I always tried to avoid paying any money up front on product, and I wouldn't care if the ticket was cheaper if I bought. Just like in the business world, real business men do not use their own money. They like to take risk with other people's money, like the banks.

For instant, I had a home boy of mines who hustled for about two years and stacked up about 1.5 million of his own money. His connect told him he would charge him $17,500 for each kilo if he paid up front, but if he fronted him the dope it's going to be $20,000 a kilo. My home boy saw the profit and couldn't resist his offer, so he bought as many as he could. He cleaned his whole stash out just to make $2,500 extra off of each kilo, and ended up back at square one. The kilos he had ordered got stopped on the highway, which caused him to lose every dime he had saved up over a brief period of time hustling.

Now he's starting all over again, and is still getting fronted by his connect. What I'm trying to say is, the drug connect is going to front you no matter what happens, so why take a risk with your own money. He could've been 1.5 million richer and still got fronted on consignment. Now he has a 1.5 million loss and he's still getting fronted on consignment. That 1.5 million could've played a big part in his out game, which could've helped start his business and he could've retired as a tax paying citizen. (Leviticus 25:53) they are to be treated as workers hired from year to year; you must see to it that those to whom they owe service do not rule over them ruthlessly. (Proverbs 22:7) The rich rules over the poor and the borrower are the slave of the lender.

Law 4- Middle men

I never deal directly when it came to pushing weight, because it's always best that you have middle men. I always kept me two to three middle men, and you should never have any more than that. I would prefer just two, but no more than three middle men.

The middle man is a person that you hand the product to, and then he hands the product to the customers. I had one head middle man that I trusted and, I would give him the product to hand to my other two middle men. The middle men would distribute the product to other dealers, which kept me from dealing with them.

I wasn't trying to take a risk of having anybody knowing that the product was coming from me. I would see other dealers in the streets and they had no idea that the product that they were selling came from me. That's how I ran my operation, because I didn't want the attention of being The Man, which saved my life.

Some dealers would deal hand to hand, and they would serve product to just about anybody who had money to buy.

That was the number one down fall for a lot of the dealers I came up with, because everybody and they mama knew they had the dope. So if you're known for being The Man with the dope, you best believe the authorities know you got the dope as well. That's why I kept a few trusted middle men, because if anything went wrong it would stop at them.

You don't throw the captain over board and risk losing control of the ship, because he's the one that got to keep the ship in order. So it's best that I stay unknown to keep the ship smooth sailing, even after losing a few crew members. I didn't believe in having a big crew, because a big crew brings a lot of charge partners. That's why you see large round ups of drug crews getting picked up by the feds, and you best believe 80% of them coping pleas.

I had a two to three man crew, and only one of them dealt with me directly. Every one of my crew members knew me by a different name, because I had I setup that way. My head dude that I dealt with directly knew me by Pistol and the other two never saw me, and they only knew me as Gates.

I had linked up with my head dude and he brought the other two along. He had been dealing with them since they were child hood friends, and they were two very loyal guys. Whenever he would mention my name amongst the other two, he would call me Gates.

I first met my head dude as a small time hustler in the streets when I was grinding grams of crack cocaine. When I got my first drug connect, he became one of my main customers. He was so loyal that I gained a lot of trust for him, and plus he was moving a lot of my product.

After a while I told him to cut off everyone and find two loyal guys that he trusted, and that's when he brought along the other two. I told him from now on I'm serving no one but him, and he shouldn't serve anybody but them. I want him to be as low as possible, because he was the only link to me.

I made sure he told the other two nothing about me, and I made sure they never saw me. They had no reason, what so ever to see me because, we didn't have any dealings with one another and I made sure it stayed that way. I would front my head dude product on consignment and, then he would ration the product out to his two man crew to distribute throughout the city.

We had a good thing going for a while and it kept me in the clear for years. I was thinking ahead, because if the heat came down on the two man crew, they couldn't tell on me if they wanted to. Gates was one of my few aliases that my head dude would throughout there, just in case his two man crew flipped on him.

Drug dealers in my city would look at me as if I was just a regular guy, and they had no idea that they were selling my drugs. To be honest I loved playing in the background, because my goal was to stay low as possible and get out the game. (Acts 19:22)

He sent two of his helpers, Timothy and Erastus, to Macedonia, while he stayed in the province of Asia a little longer. Even kings in the bible had middle men, people have been operating like this before our time. Back then they were considered as being helpers to their king, who ruled their country.

Law 5- Gun License

Luckily I was one of the few that never caught a felony, so I got my gun permit. Having a gun permit took a lot of stress on me, because I could remember riding with my illegal gun in the car nerves as hell. The gun laws in my city got street dudes shook, because if a felony gets caught with a hand gun, that's automatic fed time. So riding around with a gun as a felony was risky and, when you're in the drug game that's a risk a lot of hustlers are willing to take.

There aren't too many hustlers that don't have a felony, because most of them caught their first felony charge carrying a gun. It's very important to have gun license, because there's nothing like having the freedom to carry a gun to protect yourself in the streets. The good thing about having a gun permit is that it gives you the ups on a lot of people that carries illegal. For instant, if you're posted on the block with your gun on you and the police rolls up, you don't have to run or throw your gun away. You can just stand there with your gun on you and do as you please. Having a gun license makes you feel like you're above the law.

I went and got me the most toughest and expensive hand gun on the market, the FNH 5X7. It's best to have a license to kill, because if anyone runs up on you, you have the rights to defend yourself. You should never kill unless you have to (Law 8 self-defense), because killing is bad for business.

You never want to lose your rights to carry a weapon, because we are in a dangerous world where every man needs to protect his self. I couldn't imagine myself not having the rights to carry a firearm in a world where the motto is "to kill or to be killed". A lot of guys lost their rights to carry and I'm not saying that they shouldn't carry, because I understand why they would still want to carry if they are a felony. I'm just saying if you aren't a felony its best you go get your permit, before you get caught with your weapon illegal and want be allowed to carry.

I had a home boy that sold plenty of drugs and he ended up doing 10 years in a federal prison for being a convicted felon in possession of a firearm. I thought the drugs would have been his reason for going to the feds, not a gun. Having a gun permit is a blessing, because your armed twenty four seven and you never know when you just might have to defend yourself.

(Numbers 32:17) we will arm ourselves for battle and go ahead of the Israelites until we have brought them to their place. Meanwhile our women and children will live in fortified cities, for protection from the inhabitants of the land. Even in the bible days they were arming themselves, that's why getting my gun permit was just as important for me as getting my driver's license. The authorities will look for any loop hole to search and have proper cause to take you to jail.

Law 6- Know your laws

When I first got into the game I knew very little about the law, but as time went by I learned a lot, that helped me along the way. You'll be surprised by how many dealers in the drug game don't know their rights. It's very important to know when your rights are being violated, because the authorities are quick to break the law when their dealing with someone that has no idea what his rights are. You should never have to depend on what your lawyer is telling you, because most of the time he's in with the authorities.

I would go to the library frequently and read law books to educate myself about the law. It's best to know your laws as a free man, than wait until you're in prison and then try to read up on it to fight for your freedom. So many dealers have been railroad because they didn't know how to defend their case, because they chose to let their crooked lawyers trade them in to the system.

A lawyer will take your money and sell you promises, when he knows already that you're not going free. You will have to be the overseer of your case, because it's your life that they are playing with. So it's up to you to make sure your lawyer is doing what he's supposed to do, and is not trying to sell you out to the system.

Don't be that dummy that sits in the court room looking stupid, while your lawyer and the court is auctioning off your life right up under your nose. When they are discussing your case everything sounds like their talking Chinese, because you're not educated enough to know what's going on and what's been said. That's why you see lawyers in the courtroom whispering in the defendant's ear, and then you'll see him shake his head yeah like he understands. A smart defendant that knows the law would be in his lawyer's ear telling him what he doesn't think sounds right. Because when your lawyer and the prosecutor are going back and forth, you should be writing down all the key points on a note pad play by play that you don't agree on.

I knew a dealer got that got caught with nine kilos of cocaine, because a police officer came to his door about his music being too loud. The officer said that he smelled weed, so he arrested the guy and then searched his place and found the kilos. The guy ended get the charges dismissed because the officer didn't have proper cause to search.

What I'm trying to say is a lot of drug dealers are doing life sentences for that same scenario, because they lawyer didn't fight the proper cause and the defendant had no knowledge of what his rights were. Luckily the other guy had a lawyer that really cares about his client, which is rare because most lawyers only care about the money.

The whole point of knowing the law is to make sure your lawyer is doing what he's supposed to do, and for you to catch him in his slip ups, because it's your life that's on the line, not he's. (Romans 13:1-7) let every person be subject to the governing authorities. For there is no authority except from God, and those that exist have been instituted by God. Therefore whoever resists the authorities resists what God has appointed, and those who resist will incur judgment. For rulers is not a terror to good conduct, but too bad. Would you have no fear of the one who is in authority? Then do what is good, and you will receive his approval, for he is God's servant for your good. But if you do wrong, be afraid, for he does not bear the sword in vain. Therefore one must be in subjection, not only to avoid God's wrath but also for the sake of conscience.

Law 7 - Never Shine!

(Psalm 49:6) those who trust in their wealth and boast of their great riches. I learned that the low key dealers that never shined and stayed low as possible, was the ones who lasted the longest in the drug game. A lot of hustlers like to be seen in the exotic cars and the flashy jewelry, which will bring unwanted attention to them from the authorities and the robbers. I think shinning is one of our biggest downfalls in the drug game, because we are asking for the attention that we don't want. I think it's very stupid for anybody to be dealing drugs riding around town in a Ferrari with no legal income.

A lot of major drug crews were dismantled, because of their flashiness and their lack of staying low-key. Being at every major event and popping bottles is a bad look for any drug dealer, because you never know whose watching. Throwing big wads of money in the strip clubs is another no-no, because you're showing everyone that you got money to blow, and that's going to raise question about what you do for a living.

You want to be less seen as possible and unknown to everyone when you're dealing with drugs. You got to remember that, selling drugs is against the law and, they are giving some serious sentences out once you're convicted. I never knew why some hustlers would be surprised when they find out they're being investigated, because they should've expected that from the life style they were living.

I know most of us came from nothing and, it's hard for us to not shine when we get some money. But that attention is going to bring everything to an end real fast, so it's best to wait until you're done with hustling, and then enjoy yourself. It makes no sense at all for any drug dealer to be balling while he's grinding, that's like eating the food as you cook, there will be nothing left to serve at dinner time. Like law 9 says, "save as much money as you can", because that money is going to play a big part in your out game.

You do want to bring the attention to the robbers that you have money, because they will have you wishing you had a life sentence. I can recall were drug spots where hit and the robbers killed everybody in the spot, because the robbers aren't dumb and they know that drug dealers are capable of putting a large bounty on their heads. So why would the robbers allow the drug dealers to live, when they know that they're taking a risk of getting killed later on for the robber. That's why a lot of robbers take the robbing game very seriously, and that's why the hustlers should take the drug game serious as well, because it's a serious business.

All the shining and flossing could cause you to lose your life and your family life as well, because your actions could reflect on them. There are kidnappings going on all across the world, because dudes are hungry and they'll snatch up love ones for ransom. We all like to ask ourselves why the white man doesn't get caught selling drugs, because the white man knows out to be low key. There not in the clubs popping bottles saying "hey look at me, I'm a drug dealer", because they know the consequences of selling drugs are critical.

A lot of the white drug dealers are normal looking people that live in a middle class neighborhood with the white picket fence. You wouldn't have a clue that they sold drugs, and that's why they are successful. We as black men likes to flaunt of wealth around like we're legit, and that's bad for business.

I knew a major drug dealer from back in the day that was very low-key about what he was doing, but his crew was very flamboyant. He didn't wear flashy jewelry and he didn't have a lot of cars, all he drove was an old beat up pickup truck. This dude was pushing major weight and he could've bought a hundred cars if he wanted to, but he chose to stay low-key. One of his workers was a well-known dope boy and he had just about every car you could name, and he wore more gold than Mr. T. If you didn't know any better, you would have thought he was The Man.

One day the feds had come and snatched up the main man, and tried to get him to rat on his worker. The feds had no idea that they had The Main Man in their presents the whole time. He refused to tell them anything and they ended up giving him 5 years for a gun and thirty thousand dollars. That was a slap on the wrist for a drug dealer that was bringing in over 100 kilos a month.

The feds was so caught up in locking up the guy that was shining, that they over looked the regular guy who had kingpin status. After severing his five years for the gun charge he retired from the game, because he knew he dodged a bullet. His worker who was known for shinning wasn't that lucky, because he finally got busted a few years later and was sentenced to a life sentence.

The fed just knew they had the right man and he wasn't even The Main Man, but in their eyes he looked and played the part of The Main Man. Same way with the robbers, they chose their victims by what they drive and their flashiness. A low-key guy would go under their radar, and that's why it's important to be low-key. (Luke 12:15) And he said to them, "Take care, and be on your guard against all covetousness, for one's life does not consist in the abundance of his possessions." (James 1:9-11) Let the lowly brother boast in his exaltation, and the rich in his humiliation, because like a flower of the grass he will pass away. For the sun rises with its scorching heat and withers the grass; its flower falls, and its beauty perishes. So also will the rich man fade away in the midst of his pursuits? It was written in the bible before our time, boasting our riches as always been a big downfall.

Law 8- Avoid the murder game

(Exodus 20:13) "You shall not murder. Killing is always bad for business, because there is no statute of limitation on murder. So if you have bodies, there are no needs to have an out game, because there isn't one. You can be an old man in a wheelchair who had committed a murder 40 years ago, and they will still coming to lock you up. I have seen it many times were ex-drug dealers had retired and started their lives over, and was picked up for an old murder.

The government are soon to pass a law to release none violent drug dealers, because the prisons are becoming overcrowded and it's costing tax payers a lot of money. If it ever happens, a lot of dudes with bodies want qualify to be release, that's why I say try to avoid the murder game. The murder game was meant to cause fear amongst robbers and anybody else that tried to double cross The Man.

I figured out things could be handled in a better way, than just going around killing people to build a rep. Killing people is going to hurt you in the long run, and it's bad for business. If you have to kill someone because they old you money, then that's bad judgment on your end.

I know some will not going to agree with what I'm about to saying, but it's true. Either way it goes you're not getting your money, so it's best to just take the L. You should've never fronted anybody something that you can't handle as a loss.

Most guys that run off were fuck ups any way, and you knew it. You just thought they wouldn't try you, and now you're forced to kill him to keep from looking soft. You can always tell a loyal hustler that's not run off material, because he always buys his own and you can always depend on him to cop from you 3 or 4 times a day like clockwork.

A run off, is always a home boy that got problems and is looking for you to help him out. His whole plan was to run off from the gate because, he's going to use you to get his self-straight and then say fuck you. That's way you have to be smart about, who you chose to fronting drugs to.

Once you start killing, your name is going to stay in the authority's mouth because you've done created fear in the people that wants you off the streets. When people fear you they are quick to give your name to the authorities every chance they get, which will cause you to become public enemy number one.

The murder game mixed with drugs will most defiantly get you the death penalty. That's why I say in (Law 5) it's best to get your gun permit, so that you can buy your gun of choice and defend yourself in self-defense. You should only kill when it's in shelf-defense because, that's the only way you can beating a murder rap.

Some people don't realize it's harder to beat a murder case, than what they think. You might know a few people that's walking around with bodies under their belts, but that doesn't mean they off scot free. They got something called "Cold Case", which will catch up with you in the long run.

More people have gotten caught for murders, than have got away with them. It doesn't matter if a murder was committed 30 years ago, they will come and get you as if it occurred yesterday. Cold Case files get reopened every day, because somebody is looking to give a statement on an old murder for a lighter sentence. God does not like ugly and murder is one thing he would not tolerate. (Matthew 5:21) "You have heard that it was said to those of old, 'You shall not murder; and whoever murders will be liable to judgment. Once again, once you commit a murder there is no out game.

Law 9- Save

(Proverbs 21:20) Precious treasure and oil are in a wise man's dwelling, but a foolish man devours it. (Proverbs 13:22) A good man leaves an inheritance to his children's children, but the sinner's wealth is laid up for the righteous. Every hustler should save as much money as they can by giving themselves a $50,000 a year salary, because selling cocaine is not promising. To a lot of drug dealers that would be torcher for them, because they have lavish life styles that causes them to spend that much in a week.

I refuse to blow my money at the strip club, or buying materialistic things with no value. The idea of hustling is to stack your money and then enjoy yourself once you accomplish your goal. A $50,000 salary is what a person with a decent job would make, which is pretty good for average guy that's living a regular life. You want to seem as regular as possible to where you want bring attention to yourself.

You want to come off as a guy that doesn't have a lot, but you're still comfortable though. When it's all said and done, you will be amazed by how much money you could save by living on a $50,000 salary. It will also keep you grounded because, you want be able to do a lot of the things that would cause you to bring attention to yourself. What really matter is the fact that you know you're rich, you just want be living like it.

I can recall a lot of guys in the drug game spending more money than what they were making. They would profit about a hundred thousand, and then turn around and spend seventy thousand, which was stupid to me. Most of their money would be tied up in assets, and when the authorities come and take everything, they can't afford a lawyer or make bond.

You have to save for a rainy day or you'll get caught up in the storm. I knew a guy that had 2 or 3 houses and about 30 cars, and about seven hundred thousand in jewelry. If you didn't know any better, you would've sworn he was worth about 2 to 3 million dollars at least. When the feds raided his spots, all they recovered was about three hundred and fifty thousand dollars of drug funds.

He was one of them hustlers that liked to live off the flip, which meant he was living check to check, like they say in the regular people's world. But in his case, he was living from shipment to shipment. Whatever profit he made he would spend and then be depending on the next drug shipment to come through. What' so dangerous about that is, his connect could stop supplying him at any given moment and he would have nothing to fall back on, which would cause him to sell everything he has in order to get back on his feet.

You must save in order to have an out game, because you have to have seed money to build from. Once you get yourself established as a legitimate business man, then you can splurge as you please. It makes no sense to spend as you grind, you'll never be in a comfortable position to retire if you wanted to. The spending would cause you to depend on the drug game until you hit a dead end, which will have a very bad outcome. Not too many

drug dealers get the opportunity to retire, because of their

addiction to living the lavish life style.

You should only spend 10% of your profit and save the

other 90%. Most would spend 90% of their profit and save 10%,

because they're depending on their drug supply from their

connection. Like it say in the bible, (1 Corinthians 16:2) on the first

day of every week, each of you is to put something aside and

store it up, as he may prosper, so that there will be no collecting

when I come.

Law 10- Live a double life

Even though we like to live a flashy life as drug dealers, just about 95% of everyone who sell drugs will never admit they're a drug dealer. We like to think we're being low-key, even though are appearance is screaming drug dealer. I think all drug dealers should live their lives like super heroes, because Batman, Spiderman, and Superman all hide their identities to the public. They would live like regular people during the day, and then when it's time to get down to business they would change into super heroes. I believed in changing the myth of what a drug dealer looked like, because it's not hard to figure out who's a drug dealer these days.

They are white guys that sold plenty of drugs and you would never know they did by looking at them. They live in nice suburban neighborhoods as hard working citizens that are living a normal regular life. Their wives, kids, neighbors don't have a clue that they are drug dealers, that's how you keep others safe from your illegal activities. They couldn't snitch to the authorities to save their lives, because they would honestly not know anything about what was going on.

I made sure that the woman of my life was just as green as my neighbors were, she's a smart educated, intelligent woman that knows nothing about the streets and she hates drug dealers. Because those the type of women that will help keep the heat off of you, unlike a loud mouth female from the streets that will spread your business amongst hood friends. Those type of women runs with other women of that same nature, and that all have boyfriends from the streets, that you don't not want your business get out to.

That's why you need a classy educated woman that surrounds herself with people just like her, that knows nothing about the streets and hates guys that break the law. Once you find you a woman of the caliber you should marry her and start you a beautiful family, because she going to play a major part in your out game. (Genesis 2:24) Therefore a man shall leave his father and his mother and hold fast to his wife, and they shall become one flesh.

I knew a home boy who had a girlfriend, that was his Bonnie and he was her Clyde. He would let her ride with him when he took care of business, and she knew about everything he had going on. One day the feds came to her with photos of him eating dinner with another woman, and she got upset over the photos. The feds knew what they were doing because that's the type of games they like to play.

Once they knew that she was upset they begin to ask her questions about her boyfriend, and she told them everything they wanted to know out of anger. At that moment, she was so upset that she didn't care about the fact that she was hurting him by talking. She told everything she knew and seen with her own eyes, because she wanted him to hurt like she was.

If he was married to her, none of the info the feds got from her could be used against him. But since she wasn't married to him, they were able to use the info to send him away for good. That's why it's best to not let anyone know anything about what you're doing illegal, because they could be your key witness down the line.

Anyone close to you shouldn't have a clue about what you're doing outside of your regular life. That way they can help convince the authorities that you are a hardworking man that does nothing illegal. (Acts 5:29) But Peter and the apostles answered, "We must obey God rather than men. Even Peter felt like what man say is wrong, might not be wrong in God's eyes.

Law 11- Non affiliation

My main problem was affiliating myself with well-known drug dealers, because they were my childhood friends that I grew up with. So I had no choice but to hang out with them, but that's what ran me hot in the streets. Everyone had an idea of what I did because of the people I surrounded myself with. I was taught that you should never be seen with your drug supplier, or the people that you supply as well.

You don't want to be affiliated with a certain group of individuals, when the authorities start to dismantle their organization. I was being under investigated by the feds because of my affiliation with one of the biggest drug dealers in my city, and all we did was hang out at strip clubs together.

Most drug dealers are being recognized by the crews they hang out with, and once the authorities start snapping pictures, they have proof of your affiliation. I could be in the same room with a guy I was supplying drugs to and you would never know we knew each other, because I would act as if I never seen him before in my life. Because what we don't realize is, people are fascinated by our life style as drug dealers. That's why they love to watch our every move and treat us like movie stars. They notice everything about us from, what car we drive, who we dating, where we live, what we are wearing and who we hang out with. That's why it's not good to be seen with people you're dealing drugs with, because it will only affiliate you with them.

The feds likes to build buddy cases, they will come roundup everyone in your crew on a Rico charge. That's why I went out and got me a whole new group of friends, a group of hardworking people that does nothing but work every day. If the feds were watching me, they would see me hanging out with my hardworking neighbors, who are family men that want nothing to do with drugs or the streets.

I knew a guy that once rode around the city with his drug connect, and everybody in the city knew who he was. It's not hard to put two and two together, when you got a black man wearing a bunch of gold jewelry in a brand new Mercedes Benz with a clean cut Mexican. The feds phone line was ringing like a marathon; they had so many informants calling in with information on what they had saw.

Drug dealers like to believe that they are smarter than the average person, so they do things out in the open as if the people don't know what's going on. The people aren't dumb at all, so don't think for once that they don't know what's going on. That's why you have to play it smart because, there are some smart intelligent people watching you.

Anyone that I had drug dealings with, I wouldn't go to their kid's birthday party, their wedding, their funeral or anything else they had going on. Those types of events are nothing but photo shoots for the feds, so that they can have photos to pick you out of a line up with. I tried to stay away from famous people like, rappers, athletes and T.V stars, because those people will bring major heat to you, which will cause the feds to investigate them, as being someone whose money laundering money for you.

(1 Corinthians 15:33) Do not be deceived: bad company ruins good morals. (Proverbs 6:27) can a man carry fire next to his chest and his clothes not be burned?

Law 12- Start a small business

A lot of the smart drug dealers, would open a small business to be seen as a regular tax paying citizen. Having their own business will explain their income and, it will give them a legitimate identity about who they are in the eyes of the people. Drug dealers are known for riding around town in their expensive cars and, live in some of the most luxurious homes without any income to show. Then they wonder why the feds are investigating them for being rich, like selling dope is legal.

A small business is the first step to your out game because, that business could turn into two businesses and before you know it you'll have a chain of businesses. Once you get your business started, you should also take up a trade. Take a course in business and get you a business degree, which will allow you to have a career as a businessman. A lot of drug dealers don't have anything to fall back on, because of their lack of business knowledge.

I remember telling a home boy of mines, how I had so much respect for a lot of the old heads who owned a bunch of property in our city. They were about their business coming up as young hustlers back in the day, because they knew how to invest their money into things that were longevity. Right until this day, they still own buildings and Acers of land. The guys of my era don't own anything, but a bunch of materialistic stuff.

We need to build something that can be handed down to our kids and their kids. There's nothing like being a legitimate tax paying citizen with no worries of being sent to prison without anything to show. It makes no sense at all to have millions of dollars go through your hands and, you have nothing to show for it but a bunch of materialistic things with no value.

That's why I promised myself that I would focus on building for the future, so that I could retire from the dope game with my feet up on a beach sipping a margarita. Going to school or investing in a business is very valuable to your future, because you're setting yourself up for something better to do once you walk away from the drug game.

I got a home boy who got out the dope game and started building and selling houses. He started out buying old houses and fixing them up to rent out, which led him to start building houses from the ground up. He's now a successful business man with over 18 houses, and driving a drop top Bentley.

A lot of dealers would love to quit if they had something better to fall back on, but they have no knowledge on how to go by doing it. So they stick to what they know and, that's selling drugs until the feds come get them or the robbers kill them. (John 6:27) Do not labor for the food that perishes, but for the food that endures to eternal life, which the Son of Man will give to you. For on him God the Father has set his seal.

Law 13- have a likeable personality

In order to survive as a drug dealer, I had to make sure my personality was A1. All the bull crap you see on T.V about how drug dealers are supposed to be is misguiding people to believe all drug dealers are evil. The bad guy image is bad for business because, it only make you unlikeable to other dealers and the people in your community. You want to be love by everyone, so you have to be respectful in order to receive respect.

First you have to become a man of God and pay your tithes faithfully, because even though what we are doing is considered wrong, God knows our hearts. God looks over us while we're out in the streets hustling to feed our families, just like he looks over the people working at the sugar companies and liquor stores. Nobody really knows every single thing, that's considered to be wrong in God's eyes, but God.

As a drug dealer I was always known for my great personality and wonderful sense, because it made me a likeable person. I knew how to carry myself in public as a respectful person, and I was very polite to the elders. I would say yes mam and no sir anytime I talked to older people, and that gained me a lot of respect from them.

I remember being a small time crack dealer with two dope spots in the projects, when an older woman about 70 years old told me "baby you got to be careful, because the rent office is sending the police to run off all the dealers". That day I shut down shop and an hour later the police raided. That little old lady didn't have to tell me anything, but she took a liking to me and didn't want to see me get into any trouble.

That's why you got to do things that will make you a likeable person in your community. Do volunteer work and donate your money and time to helping the kids, by sponsoring their sports programs. The community should know you as a person that does a lot of good things for his community, and not being a drug dealer. Because you want people to care about you enough to give you heads up on the law, or become a character witness at your trial one day.

If you're that griming dude that disrespects everyone and has no respect for human life, people would celebrate the day you die or go to jail. I've seen people in their communities through block parties in memory of good dudes that passed away, because they was sadden by their death. The bad guys gets no love in the hood when they pass, it's like a regular ole day when they die. That's why you see major drug dealers in other countries being seen as heroes, because they took good care of their communities.(Isaiah 5:20) Woe to those who call evil good and good evil, who put darkness for light and light for darkness, who put bitter for sweet and sweet for bitter.

Law 14- Trust No one

(Proverbs 3:5) Trust in the Lord with all your heart, and do not lean on your own understanding. As a drug dealer in the dope game, I didn't trust anyone and my motto was "see everyone as somebody that's out to get you, that way you'll always be prepared". I didn't trust anybody, because when you're dealing with drugs, no one is to be trusted. Not only I didn't trust anyone, I also expected everyone being capable of snitching. I always felt like enough time would make anybody tell it, because everyone has their limit on how much time in prison they're willing to do.

I've seen a bunch of dudes go to trial and the people they never expected of being a snitch was testifying against them. It's always someone you never expected to tell it because, you don't give people you think will tell it, an opportunity to tell it. A lot of dudes say they'll never tell it, until they get hit with that life sentence and then it's another story. Just like you hear dudes say "man they got to kill me before I up my chain", and then they up everything when that pistol is in their face.

Back in the day dudes was lying down and doing their time because, dope charges back then was no more than 5 to15 year's max. It was nothing for a hustler to do 5,10,15 years on a dope case, now they giving dudes 25 to life and they not trying to do it. That was the feds way of breaking hustlers to snitch, the same way they did the mafia. The mafia was notorious for not snitching, until the feds start handing mobster 40 to 60 years for racketeering. Giving extreme prison sentences was a great way for the feds to get the toughest individuals to fold.

There's no shame in snitching anymore, because snitching is at an all-time high. Nobody wants to go to jail for ever, so why wouldn't they tell on someone to avoid going. A life sentence will make a man snitch on his brother, mother, cousin, uncle, and etc. So what make you believe he want snitch on you to avoid going to prison. Dudes that snitch have a lot of things they love at stake, like family, money and other valuables that they don't want to leave behind, so they would rather give you.

I had a partner that got murdered by his childhood friend that he took care of all his life over jealousy, because he felt like he was titled to have everything he had. So when my partner took him in as his roommate, his friend shot him in the head and took everything he had. If it wasn't for my partner's girlfriend seeing the dude leave the house, he would've gotten away with the murder. That's why it's important to not trust anybody, because there's no room for errors. The majority of drug robberies are setup by someone on the inside, and it's always that friend you least expect. (Proverbs 3:5-6) trust in the Lord with all your heart and lean not on your own understanding; in all your ways submit to him, and he will make your paths straight.

Law 15 – No cell phones

Everyone I know, that's serving a life sentence was taken down by wire taps, because 90% of their business was conducted over cellphones. There is no way you can avoid having your cellphone tapped. In my younger years of hustling we used payphones, which made it difficult for conversations to be tapped.

The dealers now days think they're out smarting the authorities by using throw away phones, which doesn't mean a thing if they continue to call the same phones. That's like taking medicine to cure a disease and then going back to have sex with the same person who burned you. If the people you're talking to have the same phones they been having, why call them with your new phone. Every phone you called from a tap phone will becomes tapped, so when you get a new phone and call the same people you are tapped once again.

One cell phone can wipeout an entire organization, because what the authorities do is hope from one phone to another. It's like playing a game of tag, because once you've been hit, you're tagged and then you go tag the next person, and then they tag somebody until everybody has been tagged. I done seen a cell phone tap start from a small street corner hustler, and make its way up to the connect. A street corner hustler called his supplier and then his supplier called his supplier, which led the authorities to the main drug supplier. The authorities built a case and picked up every one of them on drug conspiracy charges.

That's why I say it makes no sense to talk on cell phones period, because there's no way of getting around the phone taps. The feds don't have to do surveillance anymore, because all they got to do is hope on your cell phone and listen to your every move. They hear you say things like "I'm at the house", "I'm on my way to pick the kids up from school", "I'm at a bar watching the game". People like to tell their every move over their cell phones, so why would the authorities waste money on surveillance.

You have to get creative and find ways to communicate without using cell phones, because your cell phone calls will play a big part in giving you a life sentence. That's why they let inmates use them in prisons and jails, to make them feel comfortable discussing their business while being incarcerated. Who you think gave them the cell phones in prison, that's how you know it's a setup. It's not a coincident that there are over 100 cell phones in every jail or prison. The authorities allowed the cellphones to enter the prisons and jails to monitor the inmate's activities on the outside.

Cell phones are only used for family and friends; it's not made for anything illegal to be discussed on.

Law 16 – No dealings with Family & Friends

I learned over the years that it's not a good idea to deal drugs with family and friends, because it can cause problems between you and them. (Genesis 19:7) and said, "No, my friends. Don't do this wicked thing. It's a hurtful feeling when you fall out with a love one or a close friend over money. Friends and family members are the worst when it comes to paying you your money, because they feel like they can get away with things that others can't, just because they're family. You should never involve family or friends, because if things ever go sour, you would see the other side of them.

For instant, I watched a dope charge ruin an entire family, because of a family member cooperating with the authorities. Once that family member turned state on his own cousin for a lighter sentence, it caused the family to split up and go their separate ways. It was the auntie's own nephew, who told on her son. So she stopped speaking to her brother, who son it was, because his son gave her son a life sentence. The feud went on for years and they still haven't spoken to one another since.

That's why (Law 10- Live a double life) is very important, because nobody but you connect and your middle man should know you deal drugs. Because those are the only two, you should have dealings with. Plus it cuts out a lot of unnecessary drama that you don't need in your life. I was once told that, they can't see what you don't show and they can't tell what they don't know.

I love my family a lot and I would never want to think I have to kill a family member, just to keep from spending the rest of my life in prison. Because it's a few guys, that's been known for killing a family member for rating them out. The dope game is cold and everybody is out for themselves, so don't think for one minute a family member or a friend want rat you out. Like I explained in (Law 14- Trust no one), you have to expect everyone will tell it.

You can't put anything passed nobody, because family members and friends are quick to become jealous of your success. They will feel like they're obligated to have everything that you have, and if they can't get it, they're going to feel like you changed. I tried to avoid having conflict with my family and friends by keeping them out of my business, because the last thing you want to see is a love one sitting on the stand testifying against you. That's probably the most hurtful feeling in the world.

It's never a good idea to put any property in a friend or a family member's name, because it can become one of your biggest down falls. I had a home boy who put a luxury sports car in his auntie's name and, when the feds raided his home and confiscated the car, they charged his auntie with money laundry. His auntie was a hard working lady that has never been in any kind of trouble, but she was looking to earn some quick cash by buying the car for her nephew. After being charged with money laundry, she coped a plea deal to testify against her own nephew.

Law 17- Set yourself a curfew

I always set myself a curfew, because nothing is in the street after dark but the police and people that are looking for trouble. One of the main rules in my house is that, my doors never open after 10 o'clock p.m. I don't care who you are, you're not getting in after 10 o'clock p.m., because I'm from the streets and I know how the home invaders get down. They like to knock on your door at night and then force their way in once you open it.

I was taught by an instructor at a gun class to wait patiently in a safe place in my home, because the intruders don't know your home like you know your home. Once they kick in your door and try to locate you in the home, you now have the rights to open fire on them in self-defense. I was told that I should never go looking for them once they have entered my home, because I was taking a risk of them seeing me before I saw them.

Anybody that's trying to better their life for a better situation shouldn't be in the streets after dark, unless you're going to a real job. The streets after dark are nothing but a death trap, because the majority of homicides happen at night. The Grim Reaper likes to lurk the streets at night for random victims, why you think a lot of shootings pop off at the night clubs. When you stay in like regular people do, you'll see the after math of the streets on the morning news, nothing but killings, robberies and shootings. That's when you'll realize you made the right choice.

The reason for an early curfew is to stay low and safe as possible, because you put yourself at risk of getting pulled over at night. I went to bed early because I knew I had to get up early in the morning to handle business. I like to move around in the morning traffic, so that I could blend in with the working people. The authorities aren't making random stops that early in the morning, because they know a lot of the drug dealers are still in bed recouping from partying the night before.

I remember a drug dealer from my city getting murdered in the middle of the night. He was a young dude that was loved by a lot of people in his neighborhood, and one night he was pulled over by the police. The police had reported that they found some money and a kilo of cocaine in the car, and they suspect tried to run them over during the search. A lot of speculations were going around about the incident, which people believed that the police was trying to cover up the fact that they robbed suspect and then killed him.

That's why I say it's best to have a curfew, because when you're out that late at night it's easier for anyone to get away with murder. Because if there's nobody around to witness anything, who's going to know if you were innocent or not. When it's late at night on a dark road, a person can do just about anything they want to you. They can plant drugs on you, rob you, or, kill you. That's why you should just set yourself a curfew and sleep through the bull shit.

Law 18 – Build a relationship with lawyer

I always had a good relationship with my lawyer, because you want to feel comfortable with him having your life in his hand. I would send my lawyer money in a yellow envelope just for the hell of it. I didn't have to have a case in order for him to receive some money from me, because I wanted him to know that I appreciated everything he's done for me. I would send him and his family gifts on Christmas, birthday cards on birthdays; they got cards from me on every holiday. I treated them like family and I wanted them to treat me like family.

A lot of dealers would hire lawyers that they knew about from other dealer using them, and they would trust those lawyers with their lives. They would spend tens of thousands of dollars on one case, and still get handed a life sentence. Who can you expect a lawyer to fight for you, when he cares more about your money than do you? Your lawyer should fight for your life as if it was his son's life, that's why it's important that you build a relationship with him.

If you want to build a relationship with your lawyer, send him some sports tickets to a football or basketball game. Make sure they're the best tickets money can buy, that way he'll appreciate them. To be able to build a relationship with your lawyer, you're going to have to connect with him first. Invite him out to a bar for drinks, that way you can get him tipsy and pick his brain. You want to know what type of person you're dealing with, by seeing where his heart is. Get him to understand who you are as a person, so that he can see that you're more than just some guy with a bunch of money.

You would want your lawyer to see you as family, to where he would invite your kids to his kid birthday party. Make sure your wife and his wife becomes good friends, because if his wife sees your wife as a friend, that will bring you two closer as friends. Once you and your lawyer get to a family level, you will feel more comfortable with him fighting for your life. A lawyer that sees you as family would want nothing more than to see you free, because it would be like letting a family member down.

A lot of lawyers only see their clients as what they are, and that's drug dealers. You don't want to go to trial with a lawyer that half way thinks you're guilty anyway, because he's only in it for the money. I know a guy that had a good relationship with his lawyer, and he ran out of money in the middle of his trial. The lawyer liked him so much that he continued fighting his case for free, because he cared enough about him to want to see him free. So what I'm trying to say is, build a friendship with your lawyer or don't expect for him to fight for your life like it was his own life. (Hosea 12:6) "So you, by the help of your God, return, hold fast to love and justice, and wait continually for your God

Law 19 − Be aware of your surroundings

A lot of my friends would say that I'm a paranoid person and I would tell them that rather be paranoid, than be paralyzed or in a pair of cuffs. I always stayed aware of my surroundings, because you never know what you might peep out that could save your life. I would constantly watch my rearview mirror as I drive, and I would take different riots to my house night. I would circle my neighborhood twice before I pulled up to my house, because I needed to check out the scenery to make sure nothing looked suspicious. My family safety means a lot to me, and I would never jeopardize their live by bringing my dirt home.

I try to make sure I know every one of my neighbors personally, because if you don't know who your neighbors are, how would you be able to tell who's the police. Plus your neighbors will keep you up on any suspicious activity in the neighborhood. You would want to know if that house across the street from you has a family in it, or if it's just a stakeout spot for the feds.

The worst thing you could do is shut yourself off from your neighbors, because you're allowing yourself to have no knowledge about what's going on around you. You have to be aware of all activities that go on around you, like joggers that constantly jog up and down your street. You have to be aware of agents in disguised going through your trash looking for evidence of any illegal activity. You also have to be aware of people sitting in cars parked on your street, and to be able to notice certain cars that are constantly circling your neighborhood.

This law is not just for being aware of the authorities, but the robbers as well. You want to keep an eye out for any and everybody that could be out to get you, because it's always best to be safe than sorry. A lot of guys lost their lives and their freedom, because they didn't pay attention to their surroundings. It's very important to know what's going on around you twenty four seven. An old head once told me that he has never seen a dead paranoid man, and that stuck with me forever.

I had a friend of mine that needed damage repaired on his roof, so he made a call to a roofing company and the feds came to fix his roof instead. They were posing as roofers to look for any illegal activity that was going on in the house that they couldn't see from the outside. He had no idea that the feds was on his roof until the evidence was presented during trial. I had another friend get robbed by a pair of robbers disguised as maintenance men; they robbed him for all of his drugs and money.

It's very important that you know your surroundings, make sure you know your neighbors, your maintenance men, your mail man, etc. Whoever's in your vicinity you needs to know who they are, that way you'll know when something isn't right. (1 Peter 5:8) be sober-minded; be watchful. Your adversary the devil prowls around like a roaring lion, seeking someone to devour.

Law 20 – Never compete

A lot of Hustlers feel like they're in competition with one another, which is bad for business. Because when you're in competition, you'll do certain things out of spite without thinking about the consequences. Like for instant, if a drug dealer pulls up at the club in a new Ferrari, another drug dealer feels like he got to outdo him by buying the new Lamborghini. The completion wouldn't stop there because; the other dealer is going to buy the new Phantom Rolls Royce, which forces the other drug dealer to buy the new Bugatti. The whole time the feds is watching the both of them spend money like crazy, which is helping them build a money laundry case against the both of them. Drug dealers are so focused on balling on one another, that they don't realize the feds is in the audience amongst the spectators watching them.

Competition brings jealousy and bruise egos, because when feelings gets hurt you gain hate for that person. Once a person has hate for another person, things could get real serious, because they'll start wishing death or even jail time on that person.

I try not to give people a reason to hate on me, by living (Law 7-Never shine). Who wants to hate on a person they think is not worthy of hating on, because in their eyes they see me as having nothing, so there's no competition. While they're focusing on other dealers who have exotic cars, I'm sliding under the radar. My name doesn't even come up in conversations of dealers with money, because nobody has an idea about who I am or what I'm worth. That's why it's best to be low-key because, it keeps you out of the nonsense that goes on amongst other drug dealers.

I knew this one hustler that was all about competing with other dealers that was doing well. Instead of focusing on getting his money and get out of the game, he was caught up in out doing everybody else. This dude would take his last to make others think he was doing better than them. He went out and bought some of the most expensive cars you can name, and all he wanted was the title of having the most expensive cars out of everyone. He got that title he wanted and he also got a kingpin charge to go along with it as well, because having all those cars brought a lot of heat to what he was doing. The sad part about it is he had spent up so much of his money that he had none left to pay for a good lawyer.

As hustlers we should never be in competition with one another, we should congratulate each other on success. It's bad enough that the world is against us already for what we're doing, so instead of competing with one another, we should acknowledge one another success. Being in competition will take you out of your comfort zone, because you'll take bigger risks to get a bigger profit, to buy bigger things. (Philippians 2:3-4) Do nothing from rivalry or conceit, but in humility count others more significant than you. Let each of you look not only to your own interests, but also to the interests of others.

Law 21 – Loyalty and Respect

There's no loyalty and respect in the drug game, because every man is out for tem selves. The only loyalty and respect you should have is with family and true friends, because your loyalty and respect for them is to keep them away from the drug game (Law16- No dealings with family or friends). You can't have respect for them if you'll allow then to deal drugs with you, because you're putting their lives at risk. Plus you're putting them in a tough situation that might cause them to one day have to testify against you, if they get jammed up in a tough situation. Everybody is not build for certain situation, to where they could handle things like you would.

Loyalty is for your love ones, because those are the people that matters the most. Loyalty is looking out for family, making sure your kids are taken good care of, not screwing your best friend's wife, being your real brother's keeper. Respect is treating your wife like a queen, and treating your parents with respect. If you think that the streets is going to give you respect, you'll be waiting for ever. I don't care how many people you kill, you'll never get the level of respect you want. I don't care how much love you show your homies, they'll never be loyal.

It's easier for someone to say they're loyal than it is to show it, because everyone is loyal until a certain a stint. Like in the bible, Jesus homeboys were riding with him until the bad guys started torturing them. (Judges 8:35) they also failed to show any loyalty to the family of Jerub-Baal (that is, Gideon) in spite of all the good things he had done for them. Dudes will be loyal until their faith is tested, and once their true colors are shown you lose all respect for them. That's why I say it's no such thing as loyalty and respect in the drug game. Put that loyalty and respect towards your family and true friends.

I done seen real stand up guys do, 10 years, 15 years, 20 years, and to some people that's considered as being a standup guy. But the same dudes could fold on a 40, 50, 60 year sentence, because they've reached their limits. You got to ask your self do you truly believe your homeboy will do a life sentence and lose everything he has while you stay out balling, or would he tell on you to be free with his family living his life. That's why you should live by (Law 22- follow your instincts) and avoid the shystiness.

By best friend got murdered because he trusted a guy that he thought was loyal. He met up with the guy to buy drugs and he was found shot to death and there was no witnesses to the crime, so his murder is still unsolved right to this day. I learned a lesson from my homie getting murdered, because it taught me that you can't trust anybody when you're dealing with drugs. That's why I'm a big fan of the movie *Paid in Full*, because I can relate to it. There was no loyalty or respect in none of the old drug dealing movies like, Scarface, New Jack City, Blow, and King of New York.

Law 22 – Follow your instincts

I never felt comfortable with following another man's lead, because his leadership could be questionable, which could be a tragedy. I like to follow my own judgment and go off of my own instincts, because I know what's best for me. Never let anyone force you to move on their terms, if you feel like their decision isn't accurate with what you're feeling then you shouldn't do it. (Proverbs 27:12)The prudent sees danger and hides, but the simple go on and suffer for it.

Anytime you move to the beat of someone else drums, you will always be off beat, because you've now been taking out of your comfort zone, by giving them leadership of your situation. I remember a friend of mines telling me that he had a bad gut feeling about a certain situation, and the guy that he was dealing with was telling him that he was being paranoid. He told me his first thought was to pull off from the deal because things wasn't looking right, but the guy talked him into going on with the deal anyway. He said after they made the swop agents came from everywhere.

When you put yourself in someone else's hands, then you have no control over what happens after that. God gave us common sense to know when something isn't right, for instants he gave us eyes to see dangers, a nose to smell danger, hands to feel danger, and a gut feeling to sense danger. So whenever you get that gut feeling don't ignore it as being paranoid, because it just might save your life. Another man can't feel or sense your danger, just like you can't taste what he eats.

(John 5:30) I can do nothing on my own. As I hear, I judge, and my judgment is just, because I seek not my own will but the will of him who sent me. If you feel a certain way about a situation that you're not too sure of, that's God trying to warn you that what you are about to do is not right. You don't want to go against that gut feeling and be wrong about it, because that's the worst feeling when you knew you made the wrong choice. Some people's bad decisions cost them a life sentence, or better yet their life.

(Galatians 5:17) For the desires of the flesh are against the Spirit, and the desires of the Spirit are against the flesh, for these are opposed to each other, to keep you from doing the things you want to do. I watched a whole crew go down because of their leader had bad judgment, nobody in the crew could think for themselves. If the leader told them to jump they would ask him how high, and if he told them to kill, they would kill without thinking twice. If any of them would've thought for themselves they probably would've been in a better position, than what they are in. but once you make that final mistake, there's no turning back from it.

Law 23 – Cut off ties with all chargers

Anytime you're dealing with drugs, you should cut off all ties with those who have caught a charge. As cruel as it sounds, it will save you from a lot of stress and it will keep their heat off of you. They should understand your decision, because now that they have a charge, their now known in the system for being a drug deal. So they should understand that their situation could put you at risk, because it's only going to bring heat to anyone associated with them.

To be honest anybody with a drug charge, shouldn't want to come around anyone they care about that's still active in the drug game, unless they're working with the authorities. A drug dealer getting busted in the dope game is like a porn star catching HIV in the porn industry. You done got yourself in a bad situation, so why you want to stay around and get everybody else messed up. It's over for you, retire and let those who haven't got caught enjoy their run.

When a person catches a charge, they make others around them feel very uncomfortable. That's why it's best to keep them away from you, because it will stop all speculations that they're snitching. I'm not saying that you shouldn't help them with bond money or lawyer feeds, I'm talking about them still trying to hustle with you. Just like in basketball or football game, when a player gets injured they're out the game. You're no longer helpful to the team, so why try to keep playing.

I saw a situation where a guy was on the run for a drug charge, and his friend let him stay at one of his stash houses. An undercover agent noticed the guy that was on the run, and followed him back to the stash house. The agent called back up and they arrested the guy, but they also stumbled across millions of dollars and hundreds of kilos. What I'm trying to say is, if the guy never allowed his friend to hide out at his spot, he wouldn't have gotten caught.

That's why I say it's best to cut off all chargers, because they could hurt you in the end. They should be somewhere trying to fight their case and starting a brand new life as a hardworking citizen, because the drug game is over for them. I don't care if it's a gram or a kilo that they're charged with, because the prosecutor's main goal is to put a drug conviction on their record as a first time defendant. So that they can give them the maximum sentence on their second drug offence, that's why they should walk away from the game while they're ahead.

(Psalm 41:9) Even my close friend in whom I trusted, who ate my bread, has lifted his heel against me.

Law 24 – Never gossip

I always tried to stay away from gossip, because when you gossip it keeps you in the mist of he said - she said. That's not a good look for you when you're trying to be a person that supposed to be low-key, because you're now a part of the drama. Which could put you in a life or death situation, because some people will try to find any reason they can to do something to you?

(Proverbs 16:28) A perverse person stirs up conflict, and gossip separates close friends. Even the bible speaks on how evil gossip could become, because it makes a person that's close to you feel like you can't be trusted. For instant, I know two best friends that fell out with one another, because one friend heard that the other friend was telling everybody he owed him money. It hurts to hear gossip about you, when it's coming from a person you call your friend.

You should focus on getting your money, so that you can get out of the game. The drug game is not promising, because it's stressful and it causes you to have a lot of sleepless nights. We hustle to have a better way of life, and God gave us the strength and knowledge to be good at what we do. (1 Thessalonians 4:11) And to aspire to live quietly, and to mind your own affairs, and to work with your hands, as we instructed you,

Street gossip is the worst type of gossip, because it could become very dangerous for the gossiper. People get murdered all the time just for speaking on they heard about, because street dudes don't take that talking too much lightly. Dudes who have committed unsolved murders aren't trying to go to jail, so anyone with loose lips, they are closing them. It's even been time were innocent people have gotten murdered, because someone spread gossip that they were snitching, which later on came out to be false. That's why it's not good to gossip, because it could cost you or an innocent person their life.

(Ephesians 4:29) Let no corrupting talk come out of your mouths, but only such as is good for building up, as fits the occasion, that it may give grace to those who hear. When you speak on someone make sure it's something good or positive, that you're saying about that individual. So if it does get back to them that you spoke highly of them, it would give you a good reputation of being a positive person in their eyes. Plus speaking positive on others will get you very far in life, and people would have the up most respect for you.

There was a guy that was known for gossiping, and he would know everybody's business. If you would lesson he would tell you everything he knew, and he was known all over the city as being a big gossiper. If anybody had money, he knew about them and if anybody got shot or murder, he knew who did that has well. His name had got so bad for being a gossiper that no one wanted to be around him, because they were afraid that he would tell their business as well. After a while he became a lonely man with no friends, because no one wanted to be around him. Now he's without any body to gossip to, and is living a lonely life because no one wants to be bothered with a gossiper.

So the best way to keep your name out of a bunch of he said she said, is to speak good on a person or don't say anything at all. Plus nobody respects a gossiper, because they are seen as someone without a life of their own that likes to talk about others. (Titus 3:2) speak evil of no one, to avoid quarreling, to be gentle, and to show perfect courtesy toward all people.

Law 25 – Befriend an Insider

There is a difference between a gossiper and an Insider, because a gossiper will talk about any and everything to anybody, and half of stuff they tell you is rumors or something they made up just to have a conversation. An Insider is a person that can't hold water, but they'll only tell what they know to certain people that are close to them. An Insider will tell you things that can help you stay out of jail, because the information they give you is very valuable. It's nothing like gossip, because it takes two to gossip and gossip is just a bunch of random talk about any and everything.

An Insider likes to be very low key about the information that he gives you, because he knows that the info he's tell could get him in trouble. Befriending an Insider could save your life, because the information that he gives you is based on who got busted and who's working with the police. He likes to be paid for his services but it's worth every penny, because it's not any of that street info you get from sitting in the barber shop chair. That barber shop info is what I call gossip, because it's a group of people talking about random stuff that they had heard. All you need is one Insider that keeps his ears in the jails and court houses and not on the streets, because the court house and the jails get the info first before it hits the streets.

An Insider might have a girlfriend that works for the DEA office, or he could be related to someone that works in the county clerk's office. He has connections on the inside of the police department and he likes to hang out at bars where all the lawyers and cops hang out. He's a very clean cut person that's carries his self as an intelligent educated person that knows how to blend in amongst the right people. He has a way of getting very valuable information, like court dockets, indictments and prisoner's paper work.

(Luke 12:2) Nothing is covered up that will not be revealed, or hidden that will not be known. Drug dealer's gets busted all the time without anyone knowing about it, and they become informants overnight. So when the Insider gets wind of the info, he passes it along to someone very important that information could be helpful to. I can recall a guy getting busted and nobody had a clue, and he had agreed to wear a wire to setup other dealers. He ended up taking a lot of his close friends down, because he wasn't man enough to stand up to his own charge. If a lot of those guys had an Inside man, that would've got wind of what he was up to before he got them caught up.

(Ecclesiastes 12:14) For God will bring every deed into judgment, with every secret thing, whether good or evil.

Law 26 – Have faith in God

In order to survive in the drug game you must have faith in God. (James 2:19) You believe that God is one; you do well. Even the demons believe—and shudder! A person that has no faith in God will be deceived by the devil, because the devil will make you think that everything you've accomplished was all done by you with any help from God. You will worship money as your God and you'll live in greed until money becomes the death of you.

(Matthew 6:24) "No one can serve two masters, for either he will hate the one and love the other, or he will be devoted to the one and despise the other. You cannot serve God and money. God will look over you and protect you from those that mean you no good, but you have to give yourself to him so that he could guide you through your journey of life. The drug game is short term, so you got to give yourself to God to prepare for your out game. God is a patient God and he will accept you forgiveness for your sin.

Matthew (6:19-21) Do not lay up for yourselves treasures on earth, where moth and rust destroy and where thieves break in and steal, but lay up for yourselves treasures in heaven, where neither moth nor rust destroys and where thieves do not break in and steal. For where your treasure is, there your heart will be also. You should never worship money more than you worship God. When you die all the money you earned will be left behind, and the only thing you'll be able to take with you is your holy spirit.

A lot of drug dealers don't reach out to God until they get a life sentence, or their stretched out in the hospital all shot up with tubes in their mouth. You shouldn't have to wait until you're in a bad situation to turn to God, if you done it earlier you wouldn't be in that situation. God looks out for everyone, the strippers, robbers, killers, thieves and drug dealers, but your heart has to be in the right place. It's not about what you do, because it's all about what's in your heart.

You have to mean good even though you're doing bad things, because God knows your heart. If you made it back safely from a drug run, you should thank God. Because it's a 50-50 chance for anybody to make it back safe from a drug run on the highway.

I remember getting pulled over by the drug task force on the high way, the serve the SUV I was in from the truck to the motor. I was standing on the side of the highway praying to God, while they searched for drugs and guns. I asked God please do not let them find my 45 automatic pistol under the floor mat. When they came to me and told me I was free to go, I burned rubber as I grabbed the 45 from under the floor mat. God had once again showed me that he was with me.

Law 27 – Pay your debts

It's very important that you pay your debt, you should pay your debt before you spend one penny on yourself. When I say pay your debt, I talking about paying your drug supplier. Because a lot of dealers like to treat their self before they take care of their debt. Why would you buy a new car and a bunch of other thing you desire, and then try to pay your supplier on the backend? What if something went wrong to where you didn't have enough to pay your supplier, and now you're stuck in a bad situation? That's why it's best that you pay your supplier first, that way if anything goes wrong it's on your end.

You don't want to be seen as a screw up by your supplier, because then they want take you seriously. You want them to see you as a liable person that's serious about his business, that way they'll have more respect for your hustle. If anyone is willing to front you anything so that you could feed your family and to have a better life then you should take that into consideration to pay them. You must remember that if it wasn't for them you would be in a worse situation, instead of living a life of luxury.

(Romans 13:7-10) Pay to all what is owed to them: taxes to who taxes are owed, revenue to whom revenue is owed, respect to who respect is owed, honor to who honor is owed. Owe no one anything, except to love each other, for the one who loves another has fulfilled the law.

I remember being a young teenager getting front a half kilo of cocaine and I fronted nine ounces to my home boy, which was half of the half of kilo. I was depending on him to pay me, so I spent the majority of my profit on gold jewelry. My home boy had a situation where the person he fronted drugs to didn't pay him, so that meant he couldn't pay me, which meant that I couldn't pay my supplier all of his money. So he cut me off because he saw me as a screw up, and he felt that I wasn't serious enough about my hustle, which I can understand.

(Matthew 25:27) Then you ought to have invested my money with the bankers, and at my coming I should have received what was my own with interest. If you owe your supplier money, you should make sure you pay him a little interest on what you owe him to show him your appreciation for being patient. That way you'll make him feel like it's in his best interest if you take longer. Nobody likes to wait on their own money or wants to feel like you done messed up their money.

You want your credit to be A1 with your supplier, because it helps build a strong trust with them that you're about business. Once they know that your trust worthy and they don't have to worry about you messing over their money, there's no limit to the amount of product that they would front you. Psalm (37:21) the wicked borrows but does not pay back, but the righteous is generous and gives.

Law 28 – Move at your own pace

I always moved at my own pace, because I never believed in putting my life into anyone hands. A lot of dealers like to move in a fast pace to impress their drug connect with the turnaround, and I'm one of the ones that like to move at my own pace. Like I said before, "I'm taking my time, because if I get caught with the drugs they want take my time". I'm not about impressing anybody, because my freedom is the one that's at stake, not theirs. So why feel pressured to do other than what you feel is right, you're the one that's taking the risk.

If you want to be a boss, you have to move and think like a boss. Bosses don't take orders, because bosses give orders. If anybody tries to tell you to move product quicker than what you can move it, you need to tell them to move it then, because it's not worth your time. I've seen to many people lose their life and freedom over trying to move too fast.

What people don't realize is, dope sells its self. The dealers are just holders, because people are going to buy it no matter who has it. If you put a bag of dope on the corner it would sell its self.(2 Peter 3:9) The Lord is not slow to fulfill his promise as some count slowness, but is patient toward you, not wishing that any should perish, but that all should reach repentance.

I knew a home boy who got fronted about 30 kilos, and his connect was pushing him for a quick turnaround. He only had the drugs for about three days, and they were rushing him as if he was taking too long. The rush forced him to make some disparate decisions, because he was trying to impress them with the quick turnaround. He started calling people he barely messed with, because he was trying to dump the 30 kilos off fast. Just so happen he called the wrong dude, and they murdered him for them.

(Colossians 3:23) whatever you do, work heartily, as for the Lord and not for men. No man should be able to put a time limit on you but God, and if you allow anyone to rush you then that means you have no control over the pace of the life your living. Allowing someone to rush you could become a tragedy, because they could be rushing you to end up somewhere you don't want to be, or they could be rushing you to your death. That's why it's best for you to control your Destiney by not allowing anyone to rush you.

(Proverbs 12:24) The hand of the diligent will rule, while the slothful will be put to forced labor.

Law 29 – Focus only on what's owed 2u

As a hustler I never worried about what the next man made off of what I gave to him, because my main concern was him paying me what he owed me. When you start counting another man's pockets, you bring jealousy and greed into the situation. Once you hand someone anything to sell for you, you should only be worried about him paying you your money. Plus you should want him to make a nice amount of profit, because it would only motivate him to work harder for you.

(James 3:16) For where jealousy and selfish ambition exist, there will be disorder and every vile practice. Some dealers would raise their prices on their workers, because they fear that their workers would become richer than them. So they raise the price of their product to lower their profits, which controls the pace of their wealth. Some people fear others of doing better than them, because the wants to feel superior over the ones beneath them. They want you to be successful, but not as successful as them.

(Proverbs 14:30) A tranquil heart gives life to the flesh, but envy makes the bones rot. Having jealousy and envy in your heart will show through your character, because others will feel a negative vibe from your personality. Jealousy and envy is hard to hide, because no matter how hard you try to hind it it's bound to show. That's why you should have love in your heart to see other do well, without worrying about how much money they're making. A greedy man will allow his greed to get the best of him, because when you let money control your mind you've sold your soul.

(Proverbs 28:6) Better is a poor man who walks in his integrity, than a rich man who is crooked in his ways. You want your works to see you as someone that wants to see everybody do well, even if they're making more money than him. Because when your crew looks good you look good, because they are a part of your team. What leader doesn't want to see his team win?

As a young dude living in the projects, I use to day dream about me and my crew riding big body Benzes back to back through the city. My vision was never about me, because I wanted to see everybody around me make it. When I first saw the BMF movement I was blown away, because my man Big Meech brought my dream to life. My favorite saying was "Big Meech stole my dream, and now he's living my nightmare". I like the way he looked out for his crew, I never saw any sign of envy towards them.

That's why I say you should never monitor your crew pockets, your only concerns should be collecting what's owed to you. There's enough money for everyone to go around, because the treasury prints money on a daily bases. You should want all of your homies to get rich, who knows you might need them one day to fall back on for help.

Law 30 – Never take more than you can handle

A lot of times we be asking for more than what we can handle, trying to impress our supplier. Just like that old saying "be careful for what you ask for" and it's true. I remember being a youngster wishing for all the dope in the world, until I got older and reality kicked in on me. You soon realize that having all the dope in the world would put a lot of pressure on you, because now you have to find someone to buy it.

(1 Corinthians 10:13) No temptation has overtaken you that are not common to man. God is faithful, and he will not let you be tempted beyond your ability, but with the temptation he will also provide the way of escape, that you may be able to endure it. Pressure bust pipes, so when you accept more than what you can handle, it can cause you to be overwhelmed with stress. That's why you hear people say "God won't put more on you than you can handle", but your supplier will.

I can recall a situation about a guy I knew that was moving at least two kilos in a two week period, but it was mostly sold in ounces. He was a small time dealer that sold everything from grams to ounces out of his dope spot; he wasn't what we would call a Bird man. A Bird man is someone that's sells nothing less than a kilo of cocaine, and he didn't have that type of clientele to be considered as being a Bird man. His supplier wanted him to move more kilos for him, so they offered to front him 25 kilos at a cheaper rate.

He took the 25 kilos even though he knew he was dealing with something that was out of his league, because he wanted to impress his supplier. After about a week had went by, he had only sold two of the kilos. He had twenty three more kilos left and his supplier was calling him to see how much he had moved already, he was too embarrassed to tell them the truth so he dodged their calls. Now he's stressed out about to go crazy, because he has to get rid of the kilos. He got so dispread that he started fronting out kilos to any and everybody he knew.

Fronting out the kilos of cocaine to his friends was one of the biggest mistakes he could ever made, because the majority of the guys he had fronted the drugs to had never had a whole kilo in their life. The most they would buy at one time is nine ounces or four and a half ounces. One of them got caught riding around with a half of kilo in his car, another one decided he wasn't going to pay and went on a balling spree. One guy even cut the dope up with baking soda and brought it back to him saying he couldn't move it, now he's stuck with a kilo of trash. Out of seven people he fronted drugs to only two paid him every dime they owed him.

After a while his suppliers put the pressure on him to get the money for the kilos of cocaine he had owed them, so he was forced to do things he never thought he'll do, like kill his friends. It was either him or them, and there's no question what his choice was.

Law 31 – No Paper trail

A lot of dealers don't realize how dangerous a paper trail can be, it's one of the major things that the prosecutors likes to use against drug dealers when trying to build a case against them. As young black men from poverty stricken neighborhoods, we all like to splurge our riches once we get it. So we find ourselves spending money all over the place, we buy cars, houses, clothes, jewelry, and we love to travel. What we don't realize is, that there's no proof of income to account for any of the money we spend.

A round trip plane ticket for you and your girl could be anywhere from $175 to $1,500 apiece, it depends on where you're going. A brand new car for a drug dealer is anywhere from $32,000 to $450,000, it depends on the brand of the car. A brand new home could run you anywhere from $250,000 to $2,000,000, it depends on how big you want your home to be. What I'm trying to say is that's a lot of money to be spending without having any proof of income.

Anytime you spend money on something you're leaving a paper trail, and that trail of spent money will lead the authorities' right to you. Now you're sitting in your lawyer's office trying to figure out what to tell them, about where the money came from. You're a 29 years old dropout that never worked a job in your life, and you own $700,000 in cars, $300,000 in jewelry, and you're living in a 1.5 million dollar house. That's a lot of explaining you'll have to do, unless you got a good explanation on where the money come from to purchase those things.

That's why it's best that you save for your out game, because it makes no sense to spend money on something you'll never get to enjoy. Feds will be on you so quick you would have time to put 7,000 miles on that new car you bought. You'll be in the federal pen before you get a chance to enjoy every room in that new house. That's why it's best that you don't buy anything, until you get you a small business that can bring in the type of money that can help you buy those things. I know you're anxious to ball, but trust me when I tell you it will be worth the wait.

I had a best friend that thought he could outsmart the authorities, by renting a house instead of buying it. He paid $900 a month for rent, but he ended up living the rented home for ten years. When the feds caught up with him and took him to trial on drug charges, they brought up the fact the he paid $108,000 on rent for ten years without any income. They also brought up the fact that he bought three sets of rims at $10,000 a piece, and they showed pictures of thirty boxes of Maury gator shoes that coast $1,500 apiece. Being in court that day showed me a lot about how the feds work to build a case against drug dealers with their paper trail.

Law 32 – Make sure the Product is A1

As a hustler I was taught that good product develops a good business, and bad product will have you filing bankrupt. I all ways made sure my product was A1, because I wanted to keep my customers satisfied. A lot of hustlers would let their greed for money interfere with their product, by cutting the product to stretch it for more profit. The more they cut the product, the more complaints they would get from their customers. You don't want your customers to complain about your product, because you will cause them to take their business elsewhere.

Back in the early 80's, my uncle was notorious for cutting his cocaine. He was once labeled as The Re-rock King, because he would buy two to three kilos and make six kilos. The dope was so compressed that you couldn't break it without hitting it with a hammer. I can recall buying an ounce of re-rock cocaine from him and throwing it against the wall as hard as I could, and when it hit the wall it exploded into nothing but dust. Not one pebble or rock was anywhere in sight, because it was all dust.

Back in the day, you could sell a boat load of re-rock cocaine, because everybody was either snorting cocaine or shooting it in their veins. Once crack cocaine hit the streets it changed the game, because re-rock couldn't be cooked up. If you cooked an ounce of re-rock that was brought from my uncle, you were lucky if you got back 7 grams and its 28 grams in an ounce. That's how bad the dope was cut, and it caused him to go broke. Once everybody figured out his dope was re-rocked and couldn't be cooked up, it was over for him. Crack ruined my uncle's life as a drug dealer, because customers were expecting to get back 28 grams or more when they cook an ounce of cocaine.

Bad product is one way to cut your career as any kind of businessman short, because nobody wants to buy bad product. You want to be known for having the best product over all your competitors, because good product travels through word of mouth. I rather have a small quantity of good product, than a boat load of bad product any day. Good product carries your business and it takes it to a higher level. You should want a good reputation for having the best product, because it speaks for your character. That goes for any business, not just the drug business.

1 Corinthians 16:14 Let all that you do be done in love. You should treat everyone fairly like you want to be treated, and you should run your business from the fairness of your heart. You should never short anyone just to get a head, because GOD doesn't like ugly. The same way he gave you wealth, he'll take it away from you as well. Treat people with love and respect and they will always bring their business to you. The money that they spend with you could be all that they have, so why try to get over on them and cause them to lose everything.

Law 33- No females allowed

A lot of dealers would tell you that they would rather use female carriers as transports for their drugs, because they are mostly to not get stopped. Which might be true for them, but I think it's a tragedy for a woman to have to suffer in a prison cell for our sins. A woman should be seen as someone's mother, daughter, sister or auntie, and not as a mule that transports drugs. Imagine someone strapping kilos of cocaine to your sister or daughter, and putting her on a plane, train or in an automobile to transport.

Plus females are easier to break, so that's another reason why you shouldn't use them. I have seen it where the authorities threaten to take away their kids, unless they cooperate. There's not one female on earth that wouldn't cooperate to save he kids. Even if she doesn't have kids, she has a family that cares a lot about her that will encourage her to cooperate with the authorities.

Proverbs 3:15-18 she is more precious than jewels, and nothing you desire can compare with her. Long life is in her right hand; in her left hand are riches and honor. Her ways are ways of pleasantness, and all her paths are peace. She is a tree of life to those who lay hold of her; those who hold her fast are called blessed. Judges will show no mercy towards any dealers that uses women as transporter to traffic their drugs, because they see those who do as scums of the earth for stooping that low. The innocent women who life they ruined, reminded them of their daughters.

I had a friend who dodged a federal death sentence, because the feds was trying to charge him for the death of a female who overdosed on his product. The deceased female and her boyfriend were carriers for him, and they went into his product which caused the female to overdose. His lawyer had the murder charged thrown out, because they had no proof that he was the cause of her death. Just the thought of a young woman dying from his drugs made the judge angry, and he sentenced him to life and twenty years in the federal penitentiary.

A drug mule could earn as little as $3,000 or less for a trip. Drug lords, who commission the mules, can sometimes make 100 times more than that when selling the drugs brought in by the mules. A 2010 study by Mexican non-governmental organization called the National Women's Institute found that the number of women jailed in relation to the drug trafficking trade in Mexico increased 400 percent between 2007 and 2010.

The women are often convinced to act as drug mules and are assured it will be a quick and easy trip. The risks are not adequately explained, and, in fact, some women are even sent on missions, totally unaware that they are carrying drugs. What is even more distressing is that women continue to involve themselves in the business, blind to the consequences or too preoccupied with the chance to escape a life of degradation.

Law 34 – Never us product

Never get high off your own supply is an old saying that I always lived by, and I never understood those that did. How does anyone expect to get ahead by using their own supply? It's difficult to try to maintain a drug habit and get rich at the same time, because you'll soon become your biggest customer. Eventually you'll start using more drugs than you're selling, which will cause you to go broke.

1 Peter 5:8 - be sober-minded; be watchful. Your adversary the devil prowls around like a roaring lion, seeking someone to devour. You have to be focused when you're dealing drugs, because it's hard to be alert when you're high. You have to be aware of what's going on around you at all times, because any small slip up could cost you your life. 1 Peter 4:7 the end of all things is at hand; therefore be self-controlled and sober-minded for the sake of your prayers.

Getting high on your own supply could have you doing petty things like, trying to substitute other white powders substance for the cocaine that you had used up, which will cause you to have bad product that could hurt your business. I knew a home boy that would sell enough drugs just to maintain his high, and to re-up on another pack. If he had a day where he would use more of the drugs than he had attended, then he would cut the rest of the powder cocaine with baking soda.

Being a drug dealer and a drug user is a bad combination, that's just like being a pimp and paying for sex, or being a NBA owner and buying season tickets from another team. None of it would make any sense, so why would anyone want to be a cocaine dealer that's addicted to cocaine. A lot of the dealers think it's cool to sniff cocaine, because they watched the fiction character Tony Montana do it in the movie *Scarface*. He made sniffing cocaine a cool thing to do, because drug dealers like to act out his character in real life.

Getting high off your own supply is a sign of weakness, because having the well power to not use your own product shows you have a strong mind. Cocaine makes you very paranoid and when you're dealing drugs high, you are bound to make a careless mistake. There is no way you can avoid going to jail with a cocaine habit as a drug dealer, because your mind doesn't function the way it would if you were sober. You would have to be alert and be able to hold your composer during routine stop by a police officer.

I knew a major drug dealer that was once a very wealthy man, until his drug habit caused him to go broke. He first started snorting cocaine casually in the privacy of his own home and, then he started snorting at private parties with a female or with a small group of his close friends. He went from snorting a few grams of cocaine, to snorting a whole ounce in about a three day period. After a while he was feeling the effect of his drug habit, because he was losing everything he had worked so hard for.

Law 35 – become a mentor

Mentor is an experienced and trusted adviser. Synonyms: adviser, guide, guru, counselor, consultant trainer, teacher, tutor, instructor. An experienced person in a company, college, or school who trains and counsels new employees or students. They also advise or train (someone, especially a younger colleague).

As a hustler it's our duty to save a life from becoming what we were as drug dealers in our community, because a lot of the youngsters looked up to us and wanted to walk in our footsteps. They see the cars, the jewelry, the clothes and they think it's cool to do what we did, because the life style that we lived is a dream they would love to forefeel. Every hustler has that one youngster that they took a liking to and treated him as if he was their son.

To mentor someone you have to teach him the in's and out of the game, by letting him know that the dope game is nothing he would want to do forever. Because they could become accustom to the life style that comes with selling drugs, and not want to do anything else. Their whole life will revolve around selling drugs because, they want feel comfortable doing the things that regular people do to make a living. So you will have to take that responsibility to teach them that selling drugs is not a way to live their lives, because it's not right and its bigger and better opportunities.

2 Timothy 3:16 all Scripture is breathed out by God and profitable for teaching, for reproof, for correction, and for training in righteousness. The same knowledge that was given to you on how to be successful at getting out of the dope game, you should pass on to the next generation. Because if you don't try to help the youth understand that the game is not forever, it's going to be an ongoing situation that will continue ruining our youngster's lives.

Steve Jobs the founder of Apple (a multibillion dollar company), college mentor was a drug dealer by the name of

Robert Friedland. Friedland, who later on became a legitimate billionaire, had ended up at Reed College with Steve Jobs under wildly unusual circumstances. He was on parole from a federal prison, after he got caught with 24,000 hits of LSD worth $125,000. Friedland's spiritual attitude had a huge effect on young Steve Jobs, because he turned him on to a different level of consciousness. Robert Friedland was very much an outgoing, charismatic guy, and a real salesman. When he first met Steve he was shy and self-effacing, a very private guy. Friedland taught him a lot about selling, coming out of his shell, opening up and taking charge of a situation.

Law 36 – Quit the game!

Quit – to leave (a place), usually permanently, resign from (a job), stop or discontinue (an action or activity), and rid of. Synonyms: leave, vacate, exit, depart from, withdraw from, resign from, give up, hand in one's notice, stand down from, relinquish, vacate, walk out on, retire from, give up, stop, cease, discontinue, drop, break off, abandon, abstain from, desist from, refrain from, avoid, forgo.

People become drug dealers because it's the only profession where they do not have to have a college education to become, one of the richest people on the planet. It's also one of the only professions where people are trying to kill you and send you to prison every single day. The dope game is guaranteed to send you to two places, prison or the grave yard. The best thing you can do is stop while you're a head and use the proceeds to start you a better life, because it's not worth the outcome.

First offense for cocaine trafficking for 500-4999 grams mixture is not less than 5 years and not more than 40 yrs. If death or serious bodily injury, not less than 20 years or more than life. First offense for 5 kilograms or more mixture is not less than 10 years and not more than life. If death or serious bodily injury, not less than 20 years or more than life. Those are some serious sentences to face just to shine for a short period of time, because your time in prison is longer than your shine on the streets.

The Top 20 Richest Drug Dealers of all times: #20 Frank Lucas – Net Worth $52 Million, #19 José Figueroa Agosto – Net Worth $100 Million, #18 George Jung – Net Worth $100 Million, #17 Nicky Barnes – Net Worth $105 Million, #16 Paul Lir Alexander – Net Worth $170 Million, #15 Zhenli Ye Gon – Net Worth $300 Million, #14 Joseph Kennedy – Net Worth $400 Million, #13 Freeway Ricky Ross – Net Worth $600 Million, #12 Rafael Caro Quintero – Net Worth $650 Million, #11 Joaquin Loera AKA Chapo Guzman – Net Worth $1 Billion, #10 Al Capone

– Net Worth $1.3 Billion, #9 Griselda Blanco – Net Worth $2 Billion, #8 Carlos Lehder – Net Worth $2.7 Billion, #7 The Orejuela Brothers – Net Worth $3 Billion, #6 Jose Gonzalo Rodriguez Gacha – Net Worth $5 Billion,   #5 Khun Sa – Net Worth $5 Billion, #4 The Ochoa Brothers – Net Worth $6 Billion, #3 Dawood Ibrahim Kaskar – Net Worth $6.7 Billion, #2 Amado Carrillo Fuentes – Net Worth $25 Billion, #1 Pablo Escobar – Net Worth $30 Billion.

Every one of those drug dealers on the top 20 list made millions and billions of dollars, and most of them will never get to enjoy the wealth, because they're either dead or in prison. Just imagine if they took those millions and billions of dollars, and left the drug game alone to start legitimate business with the proceeds. It's not worth it to have that much money and not be able to enjoy it, because dealing drugs is a losing situation. Not one person on the 20 richest drug dealers list has beat the drug game. The drug game is undefeated and anyone one that gets involved with it will be defeated.

Here are a few examples of ex-drug dealers who changed their lives for the good, to become successful businessmen. (1) Robert Friedland (Steve Jobs college mentor) net worth is 2 billion dollars. He's a wealthy billionaire mining magnate. (2) Shawn Carter aka Jay-Z (married to pop singer Beyoncé) net worth 520 million dollars. He's a wealthy music mogul, sports agent, who has many other successful business ventures. (3) Jeff Henderson (famous TV chef) is a successful businessman, award-winning chef, bestselling author and a popular public speaker. (4) Uchendi Nwani (barber college owner) a millionaire, who owns the largest barber college in the country, and he's also a book writer. (5) Tim Allen (TV star) briefly turned himself into an A-list star known for doing family and kid-friendly entertainment, including winning the "Hall of Fame" award at the Kids Choice Awards in 1996 and making $1.25 million per episode in the final season of Home

Improvement. (6) Jermaine "Jay" Morrison (relator to the stars) is a millionaire that sells real estate to the stars, and he's also a motivator speaker. (7) Brian O'Dea (famous Canadian TV host) is a television host and TV producer. Brian once pulled of a 300 million dollar drug deal in the 80's. (8) Keysa Smith (successful business owner) was released from federal prison in 2010. She once made 25,000 a month selling drugs in Flint Michigan.

It's safe to say that drug dealers are better businessmen, so you shouldn't be afraid to make that transaction from being a drug dealer to a legitimate businessman. There's nothing like not having to look over your shoulders every single minute, and not knowing when the feds are going to come take you away for good. Not only do you have to worry about going to prison, but somebody trying to rob and kill you as well. Life is more valuable than just having a nice car, some jewelry and designer clothes, because you can get all of those things by being a legit businessman.

If you honestly went by ever law in this book, I guarantee by the time you get to law 36, you'll want to quit the game. There's no way in the world you can become a man of GOD, with your own business, living in the suburbs with a beautiful educated wife and family, and still want to hustle drugs. Your character wouldn't allow that, because you've become something more than what you could have imagined. 36 laws of powder is a self-guide book that teaches you how to become a better person, by redeeming yourself from being a drug dealer to becoming a legitimate businessman.

36 laws of powder, is like feeding a baby their vitamins in a Twinkie, because you're tricking them by giving them something they need, through something they like. If you tried to give them a vitamin they wouldn't take it, but if you put it inside of something they love, they wouldn't realize it until later on that you've done them a good deed. I wrote this book to teach and to show dealers

that there is a way out of the drug game and selling drugs is not their only option.

I hope this book will be a guide for someone that's selling drugs to turn their life around, and do something positive with their lives and business skills. I'm an ex-drug dealer that changed my life for the good by becoming a successful business man, and I hope my book could help do the same for someone else. Prison has destroyed many families by taking fathers out of their homes, and forcing their kids to raise themselves without their fathers.

If anybody knows what it feels like to lose friend to the system, it's me. I've lost so many friends to the dope game that are either dead or serving life sentences. The dope game is played out and, it has become anybody's game now. Anybody can sell dope these days, because the dealers getting jammed on a daily base. That's why the snitching numbers are high and the drug prices are through the roof. A kilo of cocaine has been in the high 20's and mid 30's in the south for over 8 years, which has never been heard of.

That's how fucked up the game is. GAMES OVER!